D1519113

RAPTORS

EAGLES

JULIE K. LUNDGREN

ROURKE PUBLISHING

Vero Beach, Florida 32964

www.rourkepublishing.com

Project Assistance:
The author also thanks raptor specialist Frank Taylor and the team at Blue Door Publishing.

Photo credits: Book Cover © Stephen Inglis; Title Page © Brooke Whatnall; Contents Page © Jonathan Heger; Page 4 © Timothey Kosachev, Barbara Brands, Maxim Petrichuk, phdwhite; Page 5 © FloridaStock; Page 6 © HTuller; Page 7 © Maxim Petrichuk; Page 8 © FloridaStock; Page 9 © R. Gino Santa Mar; Page 10 © Barbara Brands; Page 11 © Timothey Kosachev; Page 12 © phdwhite; Page 13 © Steve Byland; Page 14 © S.Cooper Digital; Page 15 © FloridaStock; Page 16 © R Smith; Page 17 © Bob Blanchard; Page 19 © Dave Menke; Page 20 © Stephen Gibson; Page 21 © Stanislav Komogorov; Page 22 © FloridaStock;

Editor: Meg Greve

Cover and page design by Nicola Stratford, Blue Door Publishing

Library of Congress Cataloging-in-Publication Data

Lundgren, Julie K.
  Eagles / Julie K. Lundgren.
      p. cm. -- (Raptors)
      Includes index.
  ISBN 978-1-60694-394-6 (hard cover)
  ISBN 978-1-60694-772-2 (soft cover)
1. Eagles--Juvenile literature. 1. Title.
QL696.F32L86 2010
  598.9'42--dc22
                                            2009000527

Printed in the USA
CG/CG

www.rourkepublishing.com - rourke@rourkepublishing.com
Post Office Box 643328 Vero Beach, Florida 32964

Contents

EAGLES AHOY!

Raptors, or birds of **prey**, hunt other animals for food. Eagles, a kind of raptor, have broad wings that catch winds and let them sail through the sky. Eagles can spot prey a mile (1.6 kilometers) away.

Sea eagles, forest eagles, booted eagles, and serpent-eagles make up the four eagle groups.

RAPTOR REPORT

Bald eagle wings measure about 8 feet (2.4 meters) from tip to tip. As a sea eagle and a fish eater, this kind of eagle always lives near water.

Golden eagles live in many parts of the world, including the western United States. They eat rabbits, **marmots**, and birds.

Golden eagles may reach speeds up to 180 miles per hour (290 kilometers per hour) when diving after prey.

Because feathers cover their legs down to their toes, golden eagles seem to wear boots. Other booted eagles include Europe's imperial eagle and Africa's martial eagle.

Golden eagles get their name from the golden feathers on the back of their head and neck.

Eagle feet have rough skin on the bottom to help grip slippery or wiggling prey.

Sky Pirates

Eagles have strong, hooked beaks to tear meat. They kill by grasping prey with their powerful feet and piercing **talons**. These fierce sky pirates are ready to take any chance to get food.

Bald eagles often find and eat **carrion** and steal food from other predators, like ospreys and wolves. They use less energy stealing prey than catching it themselves.

The world's largest eagles include Steller's sea eagles. Like many raptors, females are bigger than males. Females may weigh 20 pounds (9 kilograms), while males top out around 13 pounds (6 kilograms).

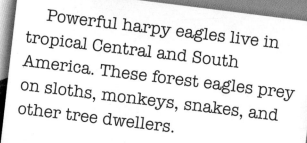

Powerful harpy eagles live in tropical Central and South America. These forest eagles prey on sloths, monkeys, snakes, and other tree dwellers.

IMPORTANT

RAPTOR REPORT

IMPORTANT

Steller's sea eagles live on the coasts, lakes, and rivers of eastern Asia. Salmon makes up a large part of their diet.

11

Eagles often eat the same prey that people do. Human fear and dislike have led some people to kill eagles.

In the United States and other countries, laws protect raptors. The Bald Eagle Protection Act outlaws the taking of both bald and golden eagles, their eggs, and their feathers. Scientists, zoos, and wildlife **clinics** receive special permission to work with eagles.

Serpent-eagles may eat carrion, reptiles, or rodents. This crested serpent-eagle hunts snakes, lizards, and mice. Their feet have thick scales to protect them from snakebites.

Bald eagles once neared extinction. Protection from hunting and poisons in the environment helped them make a comeback.

SCREAMING EAGLES

Though often silent, eagles do make a few common sounds. As an alarm or a call between mates, bald eagles may scream seven or eight times in a row. At the nest, bald eagle pairs may chitter to each other over meals.

By raising their **hackles**, eagles signal that they sense danger.

RAPTOR REPORT

IMPORTANT
IMPORTANT

Raptors communicate in other ways, too. Eagles perform swift chases and other acrobatics in the air when trying to attract a mate.

Nests and Young

Bald and golden eagles build large nests in treetops. Nests often measure 10 feet (3 meters) across and weigh over 1 ton (1 metric ton). Eagles use the same nest year after year.

Eagles need big nests so their young can spread their wings, flap, and walk around.

Golden eagles also nest on cliff ledges, as do Steller's sea eagles. The cliffs offer protection from weather and hungry animals.

RAPTOR REPORT

These bald eagle parents watch over their young one. It will get its white head and tail at age four or five.

Eagles lay two to four eggs each year. In a little over a month, the eggs hatch. The parents take turns caring for the eggs and young.

Young eagles stay with their parents for three months or more while they learn to hunt. Young South American harpy eagles stay two to three years before going out on their own.

To find out what eagles eat, scientists climb up to empty eagle nests to look at leftovers. One team found bones, turtle shells, and even a man's **coveralls** and underwear!

RAPTOR REPORT

IMPORTANT

IMPORTANT

These nestlings, covered in warm down feathers, will start to grow flight feathers at age five to six weeks. It will take another five or six weeks to grow a full set.

TROUBLED WATERS

People cause problems that hurt eagles and other birds. Junked computers, cell phones, and TVs release **heavy metals** into soils and water. These metals get into the raptors' food, collect in their bodies, and make them sick.

Eagles need large, wild places to live and be successful. People need places to live, work, and grow food. Current and future leaders must find a balance between these two needs.

20

Logs provide wood for paper, fuel, and buildings. Forests provide homes for eagles and other animals. Careful forest management and thoughtful use and recycling of wood products will help protect eagle habitat.

21

Help eagles and
other raptors by watching
and learning about them.
Take care of our shared world by
recycling and properly getting rid
of waste. Long live the sky pirates!

GLOSSARY

carrion (KAIR-ee-yuhn): the bodies of dead animals

clinics (KLIN-iks): a small doctor's office or veterinarian's office where people or animals can be taken for treatment

coveralls (KUH-ver-ahlz): a zippered suit workers wear to protect their clothing

hackles (HAK-uhlz): the feathers or hair on the back of an animal's head and neck

heavy metals (HEV-ee MEH-tulz): metals like lead, mercury, and cadmium, used in making bullets, batteries, thermometers, computers, and other electronics

marmots (MAR-muhts): large, burrowing rodents that live in western North America, Europe, and Asia

prey (PRAY): animals that are hunted and eaten by other animals

talons (TAL-uhnz): a raptor's sharp claws

Index

Websites to Visit

Soar over to your local library to learn more about eagles and other raptors. Hunt down the following websites:

www.baldeagleinfo.com
www.birds.cornell.edu/
www.hawkmountain.org
www.hawkwatch.org/home/
www.hmana.org
www.nationaleaglecenter.org

About The Author

Julie K. Lundgren grew up near Lake Superior where she reveled in mucking about in the woods and expanding her rock collection. Her interest in nature led her to a degree in biology and eight years of volunteer work at The Raptor Center at the University of Minnesota. She currently lives in Minnesota with her husband and two sons.